AMERICA LOOKS AHEAD

*A Pamphlet Series*

No. 2   February 1941                S. SHEPARD JONES, *Editor*

# CANADA AND THE UNITED STATES

*By*

## F. R. SCOTT

*Professor of Civil Law*
*McGill University, Montreal*

WORLD PEACE FOUNDATION

BOSTON

1941

# WORLD PEACE FOUNDATION

### 40 Mt. Vernon Street, Boston, Massachusetts

*Founded in* 1910

THE World Peace Foundation is a non-profit organization which was founded in 1910 by Edwin Ginn, the educational publisher, for the purpose of promoting peace, justice and goodwill among nations. For many years the Foundation has sought to increase public understanding of international problems by an objective presentation of the facts of international relations. This purpose is accomplished principally through its publications and by the maintenance of a Reference Service which furnishes on request information on current international problems. Recently increased attention has been focused on American foreign relations by study groups organized for the consideration of actual problems of policy.

# PREFACE

In January 1941 the World Peace Foundation launched a new series of publications under the general title *America Looks Ahead.* The primary aim of the series is to provide the American people with expert but condensed comment on some of the more important international issues which they are called upon to face as the result of the current wars in Europe and Asia.

This present study, CANADA AND THE UNITED STATES, is the second of the series and follows Professor Fred Alexander's AUSTRALIA AND THE UNITED STATES. Fortunately, the Foundation was able to secure a Canadian of unusual competence for the discussion of present-day and future Canadian-American relations. F. R. Scott is Professor of Civil Law in McGill University, Montreal. He is the author of several books, including *Canada Today,* published in 1938 under the auspices of the Canadian Institute of International Affairs. At present he is the holder of a Guggenheim Fellowship undertaking research at the Harvard Law School.

The Trustees of the Foundation have asked Professor Scott to survey the essential factors in the relations of our two countries and to give such interpretations as he thought appropriate. The Trustees are not, of course, to be identified with all or any of the views presented. They commend them to the reader as the viewpoint of a well-informed Canadian scholar.

S. SHEPARD JONES

*February* 5, 1941

# CONTENTS

# 1. *NEW PROBLEMS EMERGE*

The defense agreement announced by President Roosevelt and Premier King at Ogdensburg, New York, on August 17, 1940, marked the beginning of a new phase in Canadian-American relations. The United States, though at peace, thereby entered into a military arrangement with a country at war. Canada for the first time in her history made a defense commitment with a country outside the British Commonwealth. A Permanent Joint Board on Defense was set up to consider all questions relating to the security of the North American continent.

What are the implications of this move? Since modern war is total war, must not defense be total defense? Will not such an agreement extend to many nonmilitary matters deeply affecting the economic plans and political policies of the two countries? How will it affect the relations of the United States with Great Britain? Is it a step toward an out-and-out alliance or union with the British Commonwealth? Is Canada moving into the American orbit? Is this, perhaps, the "first clause of a North American constitution"?

These and other questions at once suggest themselves. It is clear that Canadian-American affairs are taking on a significance they did not formerly possess. The future possibilities concern not only North America and South America, but Europe and Asia too. Like all other political developments, however, the Ogdensburg Agreement comes out of a particular environment. It is new, but not altogether so. Many factors contributed to it and surround it. To see it in its true perspective it must be set against the historical background of Canadian-American relations, and interpreted in the light of world conditions today.

## 2. COMMON BACKGROUND OF THE CANADIAN AND AMERICAN PEOPLES

Since these are days when fundamentals are being re-examined, it is well to remind ourselves of certain unifying factors underlying North American history. Essentially the United States and Canada have common historical origins, and are fulfilling a common historic plan. The common origin lies in the fact that both countries began as colonies of western European powers. Both are the product of the movement by which the nations of the Old World set out to populate, to exploit, and to organize the vast territories of this continent. The common plan or purpose is that both countries are attempting to build the same kind of society in the new land: one based on the heritage of values inherent in western culture, and aiming at an expanding democratic freedom sustained by law. Out of a common past, Canada and the United States have been moving by parallel roads toward similar goals.

Against these common factors must be set, of course, the important distinction that the United States severed its political connection with Europe abruptly in 1776, whereas Canada has never declared its independence. Alone among the twenty-two nations of this hemisphere Canada has retained a constitutional tie, and in effect a military alliance, with the European power to which it owes its principal growth. This difference, however, though fundamental to an understanding of Canadian-

American affairs, was formerly of greater importance than it is today. For on the one hand Canada has now attained a degree of statehood barely, if at all, distinguishable from independence, and on the other hand the United States has come more and more to realize that independence does not mean isolation, and that political freedom does not prevent her from being vitally concerned with what goes on in Europe and elsewhere.

Canadian-American relations are thus at bottom the relations between two powers each engaged in the task of organizing a half of this continent in a democratic way. One of these powers, Canada, has a continuing political association with Great Britain and the whole British Commonwealth. Canadian-American relations have therefore always been—though more so in earlier days—Canadian-American-British relations. The Ogdensburg Agreement was one additional element in the whole group of these relationships. It is not mere coincidence that the destroyer-bases deal between Great Britain and the United States went through about the same time, and not surprising that during the whole course of discussions leading up to Ogdensburg, lasting over three years, Great Britain was kept fully informed by Mr. King of what was going on. Most of the strategic points on the Atlantic coast which the United States wanted were British rather than Canadian, such as Newfoundland, Bermuda, the Bahamas, Trinidad and British Guiana; there have not been any Canadian ports in which leases have been granted. The great importance of Ogdensburg in this complex picture lies in the extent of cooperation which it implies, and the political possibilities it suggests in a world situation as fluid as that of today.

## 3. *SOME BASIC UNDERLYING FACTORS*

What have been described as the unity of historical origin and purpose are two very important factors affecting the long-term development of Canadian-American relations. They go a long way toward explaining why these relations have been on the whole so peaceful and so successful. But there are other basic factors that must be taken into account. Though the course of Canadian-American relations may run more smoothly or more turbulently, depending on the changing policies of governments, the general direction of the development is determined very largely by unchangeable and uncontrollable elements. Geography, economic structure and political tradition introduce enduring factors with which government policy must reckon. The United States, as the bigger and more self-reliant partner, is much freer than Canada to alter the relationship; but she too finds her policy much controlled by circumstance. Some of the basic factors are common to the United States and Canada, and make for similarity. Some are peculiar to one country, and make for diversity. Let us look first at those factors which make for similarity of conditions on both sides of the border.

Both Americans and Canadians are living in a territory which is a single continent with certain marked physical characteristics. One range of mountains, the Appalachians, runs up the Atlantic coast to the Maritime

11

Provinces of Canada. This coast was the first settled in the two countries, has a population predominantly British in origin, and has the strongest sentimental ties with the Old World. The St. Lawrence gateway into Canada comes where the Appalachian ranges meet the great Laurentian Shield which stretches down from the far North. This eastern coastal region, including in Canada the St. Lawrence valley, is the most highly industrialized section of both countries. Beyond the Appalachians and the St. Lawrence valley lies the vast interior Continental Plain, now supporting a predominantly agricultural population drawn from all corners of the globe. The development of this great area constituted the main expansion of the nineteenth century for the United States, and of the early twentieth century for Canada; it was the era of the open frontier, of the railroad, and of large migrations. Similar problems of drought and soil erosion have confronted both Americans and Canadians in this region. Beyond the plains lies the other great North American range, the Rockies-Sierra chain, running the length of the continent and sloping down to a narrow littoral on the Pacific. On this western coast is a population which looks across to the Asiatic world, and which is increasingly conscious that North America faces the Orient just as it faces the Occident. Once the Pacific coast is thought of, not as the place farthest from Europe, but the place nearest Japan, China and Asiatic Russia, a single strategic idea begins to unite everyone from Alaska to California.

In the sphere of economics, both countries are seen to have passed through the same stages of capitalist growth and change. The period of small-scale industry is over and politics and economics are becoming more and more interrelated. Power production, the large industrial unit,

12

concentration of ownership and control are to be found in marked degree on both sides of the border. In some respects the process has proceeded further in Canada, where the smaller size of the economy and a less active public opposition to trusts and combines have resulted in an even more centralized economic grouping. Industrialization has been accompanied by protective tariffs, the adjustment of which has for over a century been a major matter for discussion between the United States and Canada. The growth of industrialism has also forced to the front the problems faced by agriculture in the changing economy. The disequilibrium between agricultural and other commodity prices, the disposal of agricultural surpluses and the financing of accumulating farm debts, are as familiar to Canadian as to American legislators and economists. In both countries the population, once predominantly rural, is now predominantly urban or suburban.

Over the whole of North America the frontier stage of growth is past. No longer can the immigrant or the enterprising lad from the populous East go out and settle on new land, knowing he can make a home for himself. The good lands are already filled. Despite the small population in Canada's vast West, the most recent soil surveys show remarkably little remaining acreage that is not marginal or submarginal land. Canada has recently been developing one new agricultural area, in the Peace River district, and has opened new frontiers through the discovery of the mineral resources of the Laurentian Shield, but neither of these movements can absorb many settlers. Both in the United States and Canada the primary question is not how to settle new country, but how to organize and improve what is already settled.

13

Canadians, indeed, are wondering whether their share of the world wheat market is ever going to be large enough again to justify the number of farmers now dependent on wheat export for a livelihood.

The similar stages of economic development have produced similar problems of social security in Canada and the United States. Unemployment insurance and relief, the regulation of wages and hours of labor, old-age pensions, housing schemes, public health measures—these until the outbreak of war have been the prime consideration of public authorities and the chief debating points of political parties. Mr. Roosevelt's New Deal of 1933 was followed in Canada by Mr. Bennett's "New Deal" of 1935, the main difference being that Canadians put theirs in quotations to show it was not original. And as both countries have a federal type of constitution, the same problem of states' rights versus federal authority has emerged in both (though more acutely in Canada owing to a less liberal attitude in Canada's highest court, the Privy Council in England) and the same kind of battle has been fought in the courts between the old legal concepts and the new social ideas. The philosophy of what is called the "social service state" is steadily replacing the old *laissez-faire* philosophy. Farsighted groups in both countries are already discussing the further development of the social service state into the democratically planned economy—a process which the war is vastly accelerating. In proportion as this idea of planning spreads, the possibilities of Canadian-American cooperation become more evident, for obviously more can be achieved when two neighbors plan together than when they plan separately.

The most important common factor underlying Canadian-American relations today, however, is the new danger from abroad which both countries are facing. Cooperation comes easily when there is a shared anxiety, and the United States and Canada see all too clearly the growth of world forces which threaten their security. The challenge comes both on the physical and on the ideological plane. It is not only that in Europe and Asia there exist strongly armed powers engaged in programs of aggressive expansion. It is not only that in military terms such aggression will, if successful, place the United States and Canada at an enormous disadvantage by comparison with the distribution of power in times past. Basically the threat is to the inner philosophy, the democratic tradition and the whole standard of human values on which Canadian and American society has been reared. Millions of men are being taught, and believe, that democracy is finished, that dictatorship provides a superior system of government, and that the individual life is valueless except in so far as it makes itself a tool in the hands of the national leader. There have always been such ideas in the world before; but never have they been so aggressively promoted, and never before have they been so armed, through modern weapons and modern modes of communication, with the power to act on a world scale.

This fact changes greatly the ideological basis of Canadian-American relations. In earlier times international relationships made Canadians and Americans occasionally hostile to each other. On the one hand Americans looked upon Canada as the outpost of the European power, Great Britain, against whom they had had to struggle to win and to preserve their independence. On the other hand Canadians have seen in the United States the potential threat of forcible annexation. The only times American troops have invaded Canada, since

15

the end of French power on this continent, were during the American Revolution and the War of 1812, both occasions on which the cause of conflict was not Canadian-American relations so much as American-British relations. For Americans a fight against Britain meant a fight against Canada. As late as the Civil War British influence was still a danger to American unity, and out of the ill-feeling of those days came the Fenian raids on Canada. American exponents of "manifest destiny" also added their occasional threats of northern expansion, and Canadians had to look to London for diplomatic aid. All that is now old history, although traditional antipathies still survive in certain quarters. The rise of other powers to the first rank, such as Germany and Japan, has changed Great Britain from being the principal external power which might injure American interests on this continent, to being the principal external power which can help to protect those interests against the new threats. The British fleet that once burned Washington now helps to protect Washington by its mere existence, apart from any alliance or agreement. The changed world situation compels all North Americans to accept new orientations of policy. Old habits of mind must give way before the new realities. In particular the external danger forces Americans and Canadians to revise their ideas of home defense, and to think in terms of the whole continent and its adjacent islands, if not of the whole hemisphere. Seen thus, the military boundary runs north and south beside the ocean shores, and not east and west along the 49th parallel of latitude.

## 4. *MAIN DIFFERENCES BETWEEN CANADIAN AND AMERICAN CONDITIONS*

### CANADA A SMALL POWER

Perhaps the most striking difference between the United States and Canada is their great contrast in power. On the map Canada looks as big as her southern neighbor; actually she is bigger than the United States plus Alaska by some 100,000 square miles. In terms of frontiers to defend, the huge geographical area of Canada should not be forgotten. But the United States population is 131 millions, whereas in the whole of Canada there are only 12 million people. Moreover this 12 million is anything but compact. It is spread in a long thin line along the American boundary. Half the Canadians live within 100 miles, and 90% within 200 miles, of this border. The real shape of Canada, as a social and economic unit, is that of a ribbon edging the unoccupied wastes to the north. It is not even a continuous ribbon, for it is cut into four main sections: first by the northern projection of the Appalachians and the Maine boundary, which cuts off the three Maritime Provinces (Nova Scotia, New Brunswick and Prince Edward Island) from easy access to central Canada; then by the 800 miles of barren country caused by the meeting of the Laurentian Shield with the Great Lakes, which cuts off central Canada from the western prairies; and then by the Rockies, which separate the prairies from the Pacific coast. These sections are tied together by three trancontinental railroads and one transcontinental airline, as well as, in summer, water routes and highways (though it is noteworthy that no motor road connects eastern and western Canada); but even modern communications cannot overcome the strong regional interests and feelings in a population so distributed. The United States has its regionalism too, but not so accentuated, for it has depth as well as breadth, and a north-south flow as well as an east-west one. Canada has no south of her own, and while her north land is romantic in its vastness, and rich in forest and mineral resources, few people are likely to live in it permanently.

Hence Canada is a small, widely spread population in a big land. The United States has a big population in a big land. The national income of the United States in 1939, for instance, was some 70 billion dollars a year; of Canada about 4.4 billions. American wealth and power mean American leadership in this continent and hemisphere. If the United States does not assume the major role and major burden in continental defense, Canada cannot do so, though Canada has an important and essential part to play.

This sharp contrast in the size of the two countries, however, needs toning down in several particulars. Canada as part of the British Commonwealth is a larger power than Canada considered by herself. Most of the important negotiations between the United States and Canada during the late eighteenth and nineteenth centuries, and indeed up to the World War of 1914, were conducted by British officials representing the British government as well as the Canadian government, and when

18

Canadians took part they spoke with the weight of Britain behind them. Washington therefore always felt it was dealing, not with a few million Canadians, but with a great world power whose territory included Canada. On several occasions Canadians have felt that in these negotiations the interests of Britain were more carefully protected than were the interests of Canada, and this has been one of the influences making for the growth of Canadian self-government. A landmark in the evolution of Canada's statehood was in 1923, when Ottawa insisted that Canadians alone should represent her in negotiating the new Halibut Treaty with the United States. Today Canada has her own Minister at Washington, and it is quite accepted in London that she conducts all her own affairs through her own representatives when she has to talk with American officials. But a constitutional tie with the Commonwealth still remains, and because of this American agreements with Canada are on a different footing from American agreements, say, with Mexico. It is part of the understanding between the members of the Commonwealth, established at the Imperial Conference of 1930, that whenever one of them is conducting diplomatic negotiations with an outside power on a matter likely to interest the other members, it will keep them informed. Thus, as has been said, Mr. King kept London informed of all the discussions leading up to Ogdensburg. Because of this Commonwealth interrelationship, Canada represents more than herself alone when she treats with the United States.

In another respect Canada is a bigger power than she appears. Her industrial development is remarkable, considering her geographical handicaps. In 1937 she ranked sixth among the nations in total world trade. She has greatly enlarged her productive capacity since the outbreak of the war. Her importance to the United States economy is reflected in the fact that total trade between Canada and the United States is fully four-fifths as large as the total trade between the United States and all Latin American countries put together. Canada is normally America's best customer; in 1940 she bought from the United States goods worth approximately, $750,000,000 or over $2,000,000 a day. The United States has more money invested in Canada than in any country in the world. Canadians possess about 90% of the world nickel supply, besides large deposits of precious and base metals. In many respects Canada is a richly endowed country, and she can be a very powerful ally of the United States despite her small population.

## Canadian Dependence on World Trade

The common geographic features of the United States and Canada have already been pointed out. There are also certain important geographic differences which help to explain why the two countries are not one. Canada is not quite such an arbitrary shape as may appear from seeing the boundary line cut across the Appalachians, the plains and the Rockies. The Great Lakes, with the St. Lawrence and connecting rivers, do provide a special formation in this part of the continent. This huge river system, offering easy access to the interior as far west as the prairies, and linking the northwest with the Atlantic provinces, gives a certain geographic justification to the political and economic boundary. There are some natural east-west lines as well as north-south ones in Canada.

The trade of Canada has moved east and west along the St. Lawrence waterways ever since the country was first discovered. The canals and railways of today supplement the river traffic. Canadian economic development has largely been a process of opening up more and more resources in the interior and bringing them out to the markets of the world. The home market also has steadily developed, but production of the important basic commodities has always been far ahead of home consumption. A striking difference between the Canadian and American economies today is that whereas the United States exports normally about 10%, Canada exports around 30% of her total net production. It has been estimated that between the years 1927 to 1937 the exports of goods and services (including tourist expenditures) accounted for from 23 to 35% of the Canadian national income. The whole Canadian economy is thus extremely dependent on world trade and world conditions; more so than is the American economy, though some sections of America—such as the Cotton Belt—do depend very largely on foreign trade. The hypothesis on which Canadians have built their country is that there will always be an outside market to absorb a large surplus production, and to pay for the huge overhead investment in factories, railways, canals and dockyards which make that production for export possible. So far—with some bad periods—the hypothesis has worked, and by this method Canada has climbed to the high place she holds among the world's trading nations. Today Canadians are asking themselves how much of the international trade they require can survive the present conflict, particularly if totalitarian economic ideas, now increasing even among the democracies, should become permanent.

Some statistics of Canada's foreign trade will make this position clearer. The following table shows the distribution of that trade in the three fiscal years preceding the present war:[1]

## CANADIAN IMPORTS
### (In millions of Canadian dollars)

| | 1937 | 1938 | 1939 | % of total trade 1937 | 1938 | 1939 |
|---|---|---|---|---|---|---|
| From the United States | 393.7 | 487.3 | 412.5 | 58.6 | 61.0 | 62.7 |
| From the United Kingdom | 129.5 | 145.0 | 115.6 | 19.3 | 18.2 | 17.6 |
| From all other British Empire | 68.6 | 88.2 | 65.1 | 10.2 | 11.0 | 9.9 |
| From all other foreign countries | 80.0 | 78.6 | 65.0 | 11.9 | 9.8 | 9.9 |

## CANADIAN EXPORTS
### (In millions of Canadian dollars)

| | 1937 | 1938 | 1939 | % of total trade 1937 | 1938 | 1939 |
|---|---|---|---|---|---|---|
| To the United States | 435.0 | 423.1 | 375.9 | 41.0 | 39.6 | 40.6 |
| To the United Kingdom | 408.0 | 409.4 | 325.5 | 38.4 | 38.2 | 35.1 |
| To other British Empire | 87.6 | 108.0 | 102.8 | 8.3 | 10.1 | 11.1 |
| To other foreign countries | 130.6 | 129.7 | 122.8 | 12.3 | 12.1 | 13.2 |

Canada's percentage trade by continents for the fiscal year 1939 is as follows:[1]

| | Imports | Exports |
|---|---|---|
| North America | 65.3 | 43.5 |
| United States | 62.7 | 40.6 |
| Other | 2.6 | 2.9 |
| Europe | 23.4 | 43.3 |
| United Kingdom | 17.6 | 35.1 |
| Other | 5.8 | 8.2 |
| South America | 3.3 | 1.4 |
| Asia | 4.9 | 3.9 |
| Oceania | 2.3 | 5.7 |
| Africa | 0.8 | 2.2 |

[1] All figures from *Canada Year Book*, 1940.

22

Canada has been a rich field for foreign investment. To develop her industrial plant and transportation system she borrowed from abroad; first principally from Great Britain, and after 1914 from the United States. She ranks, indeed, first among world debtors (Germany possibly excepted). In 1937 the capital invested in Canada by other countries was as follows:

| | |
|---|---|
| United States | $3,932,000,000 |
| Great Britain | 2,685,000,000 |
| Others | 148,000,000 |
| *Total* | $6,765,000,000 |

Against this indebtedness must be set Canadian investments abroad (1937) of approximately $1,757,900,000, of which over a billion dollars was in the United States. On balance there is some five billions on which Canada must pay interest out of the profits of her export trade.

Certain things about these figures need to be emphasized.

First, we see that from the economic point of view Canada is more closely tied to North America than to any other continent, both as regards total trade and total investment. The United States ranks first in importance among individual countries; that is why American tariff policy is of such particular concern to Canadians.

Secondly, we see that the United States and Great Britain between them account for about 80% of Canada's total trade and for almost all her indebtedness. Canadian economic and fiscal policy is dominated by the necessity of maintaining good relations with both Britain and America and easy access to both markets.

Thirdly, if we examine Canada's trade with the United

States and the United Kingdom we see that she buys more from the United States than she sells to her, and sells more to Britain than she buys from her. Over the whole British Commonwealth, Canada sells more than she buys. In time of war Canada's unfavorable balance of trade with the United States and favorable balance with Britain are accentuated, for Canada then buys more from the former to speed up her war effort and sells more to the latter in the form of munitions of war. Under normal circumstances a good part of this triangular trade is financed by Canada changing her pounds sterling credits into American dollars to pay the American debts. In wartime when currencies are rigidly controlled, as today when Britain has created a "sterling bloc" of which Canada is not a member, such a purchasing of dollars with sterling becomes impossible. At once Canada's dependence on both countries becomes very clear, for she now finds herself with plenty of sterling with which she is unable to liquidate an accumulating dollar deficit. We shall look further into the implications of this problem when discussing the meaning of the Ogdensburg Agreement.

Fourthly, if Canada's imports are classified we see that she must import large quantities of such vital necessities as coal, oil, cotton, rubber, tin, manganese, steel and iron. Canada has great resources of raw materials, but, partly because she is a northern country, there are large gaps in those resources. Her industrial system can never be self-supporting.

Fifthly, the very reason for Canada's industrial strength—her large foreign trade—becomes a source of weakness if the hypothesis of continuing external markets proves false. Whenever world trade is violently dislocated, through economic depression as in the 1930's, through war or through prohibitory tariffs, Canadians suffer a drastic decline in their national income. They cannot maintain their present social system in a world ruled by autarchic ideas. If the European markets alone should ever be closed, even temporarily, Canadians would face unemployment and financial collapse on an immense scale. They would be forced to turn to the United States for salvation. Thus Canada's military power, her capacity to make modern instruments of war and to pay for them, is a function of her external trading power. Destroy her foreign trade, and you pull down her military establishment. If the United States is interested in Canada as an ally for defense of North America, she has to be interested in Canada as a trading nation.

The present situation with regard to Canadian wheat is a good example of this truth. Canada greatly expanded her wheat production—as did the United States—during the 1914 World War. The growing, transporting and financing of the wheat crop has long been one of Canada's major economic activities. The three prairie provinces depend very largely upon it, and all other parts of the country are affected by it. In 1939 it ranked after newsprint and gold as Canada's third largest commodity export. World prices and world markets are all-important to this business. World prices collapsed at the beginning of the 1929 depression, and Canada has been struggling ever since with a serious price problem, necessitating federal assistance to the western producers. Now many former markets have been closed by the war. The continent of Europe is blockaded. England can absorb only part of the export surplus. To a considerable wheat carryover already in Canada has been added in 1940 a bumper crop of over 550,000,000 bushels. The result is that

Canadians literally cannot find storage space for the amount of wheat, some 800,000,000 bushels, which they have on hand. Meanwhile farmers must live. Because of the nature of the prairie lands there is no easy way out through mixed farming. The rest of the economy must help to carry the wheat grower or he will starve amidst his plenty. Already Canada's war effort is being affected by this pressing need.

## POLITICAL BACKGROUND

Now let us turn to some of the more important political factors which explain differences of outlook in the United States and Canada. Ever since the sharp break with Europe in 1776, the United States has had a firmly rooted policy of avoiding European commitments. On a very few occasions she has been willing to intervene in Europe but she has avoided anything in the nature of continuing commitments. Canadians, on the other hand, have not made such a break and so have the opposite tradition. Their constitutional tie with Great Britain has meant in effect a continuing policy of military alliance with her, the understanding being that the extent of Canada's military participation, the number of men sent overseas and so forth, would be decided by the Canadians themselves. But Canadians have been just as isolationist as the Americans in situations where Great Britain was not involved to the point of war; in the Far East, for example. They have been more isolationist than the Americans toward Latin America. They have even kept aloof, though being ultimately involved, from specific British commitments on the continent of Europe, such as the Locarno Treaty of 1925 or the guarantee to Poland in August 1939. Canada has been, it is true, a member of the League of Nations, and has taken a minor share in its work; but she always expressed her objection to any idea of the League becoming a super-state with power to compel its members to act. When Canada did take a stand at Geneva she was never out of line on any major issue with British policy. What distinguishes Canadians from Americans in respect to foreign entanglements is not that Canadians have a deeper feeling for humanity in general, or any stronger impulse to aid the distant victims of aggression, but simply that Canadians are members of a political organization, the Commonwealth, which has interests and ultimately commitments in every part of the world. And as has been pointed out already, the more American policy runs parallel with that of Great Britain, and the more Canadian policy runs parallel with that of America, the less evident this difference between Canadians and Americans becomes.

In so far as French Canadians are concerned, they are more like Americans in this sense, that they too experienced a violent breach with their European connection. The cession of Canada to Great Britain by France in 1763 was for the French Canadians, from certain points of view, comparable to the effect of the Declaration of Independence upon the American colonists. It cut them off from Europe, and left an inevitable antipathy to England. That antipathy has been greatly mitigated in Canada by the subsequent guaranteeing of the French laws, the Roman Catholic religion and the French language, by the growth of Dominion status, and through the recapture by French Canadians of an increasing political influence under Canada's democratic federal constitution. French Canadians now constitute 30% of Canada's population, and no federal government can achieve office or survive without considerable support from them.

It might be thought that the British conquest of Canada would have left in Quebec a sentimental tie with France; but this was largely destroyed, though never entirely so, by the anti-Catholic trend in France during the Revolution and afterwards. The French were thus cut off from Europe both by political change and by religious trends, and this has been at the basis of their leaning toward a non-interventionist policy for Canada. French influence is likely to revive in Quebec, it may be noted in passing, if the authority of the Catholic Church should continue to expand in France as a result of the collapse of the Republic; Ottawa now has the only Commonwealth representative of the Vichy government. The French Canadians have known, also, so long a struggle to preserve their race and culture from assimilation by their Protestant and Anglo-Saxon environment, that they feel an adequate outlet for their idealism and sacrifice right at their own door. Hence in Canadian politics the contrast, sometimes the conflict, between French-Canadian nationalist opinion and what is called the Imperialist tradition among certain British Canadians, can always be seen, though the racial lines of this conflict are blurred today by the fact that an increasing number of British Canadians also think of themselves as nationalists.

During the World War, in 1917, this conflict reached the breaking point when a Dominion government attempted to enforce in Quebec conscription for overseas service. Since that experience all political parties in Canada, including even the Conservative party which is most avowedly pro-British, have abandoned conscription for overseas service as part of their programs. The French

28

Canadians on their side recognize that a minority has certain obligations to the society of which they are a part, and both in 1914 and 1939 accepted the interventionist policy with little opposition. Mr. King introduced a conscription measure to Canada after the fall of France in 1940, but this applied only to home defense and requires merely thirty days of military training.[1] All Canadian forces in England today are volunteer. By drawing the line between overseas service and home defense Canadian unity is not now endangered by conscription as it was in the last war, and in fact numbers of French Canadians have enlisted for service abroad, while their leaders are giving full support to the war effort.

This French-Canadian sentiment, while it tempers the pro-British enthusiasm of the Imperialists in Canada, has been a strong support for Canadian independence from the United States. The French Canadians have felt that their special privileges are more secure in Canada as part of the Commonwealth than they would be if Canada became a few extra states in the American Union. French refusal to become a "fifth column" in Canada during the American invasions of 1775 and 1812 was partly responsible for the continued survival of Canada. French-Canadian leaders observe that the French Canadians in New England tend to weaken as an ethnic group, finding it not so easy to preserve their language and their religion. The United States has the common school and the "melting-pot" theory of Americanization; whereas in Canada there are separate religious schools (though not in all provinces) and the dual English-French culture is generally accepted as basic to the nature of Canadian federalism. It is only the "foreigners" in Canada, i.e. the non-Brit-

[1] On February 3, 1941, a change to a four-months' period was announced.

29

ish, non-French immigrants, who are expected to "melt".

It seems true to say, however, that while the French Canadians prefer their Canadian status to annexation, they have no positive feeling of dislike toward the United States that is very different from their dislike of absorption by English Canada. More of them have migrated from Quebec to New England than to other parts of Canada. Catholic influence in the United States has grown in recent years, and the Pan American policy, which is non-interventionist toward Europe and links North America more closely with Latin and Catholic peoples to the south, is attractive on many grounds to French Canada.

There is another factor in English-speaking Canada which has greatly affected Canadian-American relations. This is the United Empire Loyalist tradition. The Loyalists who fled the States after the War of Independence were numerous enough to found two new provinces in Canada—New Brunswick and Ontario. Canadians of Loyalist stock, having suffered for their political convictions, have always prided themselves on their specially British viewpoint, and not unnaturally have been generally anti-American—often more so than the later British immigrants who simply left the motherland to find a new home in Canada. At the same time these Loyalists played a great part in democratizing Canada by bringing in American ideas of self-government to still undeveloped colonies.

In recent years the growing strength of the Pan American movement has emphasized Canada's isolation from the other peoples of this hemisphere. The trade figures quoted above show the small fraction of Canadian trade going to Central and South America. Membership in the British Empire, and later in the League of Nations, gave

Canada political ties with outside powers—including, in the League, the Latin American republics—which made the hemispheric idea appear somewhat strange and unimportant. As the political situation grew worse in Europe during the 1930's, the desirability of a strong regional collective system in the Americas began to strike many Canadians, and the first demands that Canada take part in Pan American conferences were heard. In 1938 Mr. J. S. Woodsworth, the leader of the Cooperative Commonwealth Federation (Canada's Farmer-Labour Party) suggested to Mr. King that Canada should have a representative at the Lima Conference, but the Premier refused on the grounds that Canada had not been invited, that the constitution of the conference permitted only "republics" to attend, and that in any case public opinion in Canada was not sufficiently "informed and mature" to warrant such a step (speech of March 30, 1939). To many Canadians not yet accustomed to the idea of Canada acting independently, a move toward Pan Americanism seemed necessarily to involve a move away from Britain, particularly if made during the critical European situation. Hence Canada was not officially represented (though the first unofficial Canadian observer was present) even at Havana in 1940, where matters of the greatest concern to Canada and to the British Commonwealth were under consideration. Canadians often think of their country as being an interpreter between Great Britain and the United States, but they have not thought of extending that role to include interpreting the Commonwealth to the Americas.

However it seems clear that circumstances are forcing Canadians in the direction of closer association with the hemispheric group of nations. In 1940 Ottawa sent a special trade mission with a Cabinet Minister to South America to see what markets might be available for Canadian goods now barred from Europe, and though it did not go beyond the West Indies owing to the illness of its leader, it revealed the growing interest. Mr. King has also announced the creation of two new Canadian Legations, one in Brazil and one in the Argentine—the first for South America. The problem of surplus wheat in Canada makes the work of the Inter-American Economic and Financial Advisory Committee, which deals with the question of surplus commodities in this hemisphere, particularly important to Canada at the present time. President Roosevelt's pledge that the United States "will give economic support, so that no American nation need surrender any fraction of its sovereign freedom to maintain its economic welfare", will hearten producers on the prairies as well as on the pampas. Moreover Canada is directly concerned in the defense of Newfoundland; the United States has acquired a naval base there, as one of the leased British bases; all these bases, Secretary Cordell Hull has announced (September 7, 1940) are now open, under the cooperative arrangements agreed upon at Havana, to the other American republics. Pan Americanism has thus come right up to Canada's front door, and she can scarcely continue to ignore it.

## CANADIAN NATIONAL SENTIMENT

Finally, to conclude this brief survey of basic factors affecting Canadian-American relations, the growing sense of nationality among Canadians must be noted. Canada will never produce a narrow racial nationalism, because of her dual English-French social base and the mixed nature of her immigrant population. She can attain and has developed, however, a national control over her own economic and foreign policies, and with it a national consciousness. Her economic self-government is complete. As far back as 1859 she achieved the right to an independent tariff policy, free to tax even British goods, and in 1878 she adopted a national policy of protection of home manufactures. Her growing industrialization brought increasing competition with British manufacturers, and despite the Imperial Preference system begun in 1898 the Canadian market has never been easy of access to British goods. Since the break-up of the old colonial system in the 1840's the British Empire has never had a centralized economic policy. At the Ottawa Conference of 1932 an attempt was made to increase the self-sufficiency and economic interdependence of the Empire countries, but this attempt had to give way before both British and Canadian needs for freer relations with outside countries. The Canadian-American trade agreements of 1935 and 1938, and the British-American treaty of 1938, marked the decline of the Ottawa closed-Empire concept. The unnatural character of this concept in the modern world was soon shown by the war, when Canada found herself outside the sterling bloc—financially a foreign country— and Great Britain had to disregard Empire economic ties in her need for allies in Europe and the Near East. Canadians are closely linked to the British Empire markets and the American market by history and proximity, but her tariff and exchange policies are decided by herself.

Similarly a political nationalism has developed in Canada during the past century. It has shown itself through the gradual extension of Canadian self-government over the whole field of domestic and foreign policy. Canadians took the lead in the achievement of responsible government at home (1848) and of Dominion Status within the Commonwealth (1926). By the Statute of Westminster of 1931, a British statute dealing with the legal powers of the Dominions, it was laid down that any British Dominion was free to make laws on any subject whatever, regardless of whether they conflicted with British laws on the same subject; this was intended to get rid of the obsolete doctrine, still law until 1931 (and still law today for Australia and New Zealand which have not adopted the Statute of Westminster) which gave legal supremacy to British laws over Dominion laws whenever they conflicted. Thus Canada may now make what laws she pleases.

There are still, it is true, relics of colonialism in the Canadian constitution, in the fact that Canada cannot amend her own constitution without asking the British Parliament to make the change, cannot decide finally her own lawsuits in her own Supreme Court but must resort to the Privy Council in England, and may theoretically have any of her laws vetoed by the King. Up to the outbreak of war in 1939, too, it was held by most Canadians that Canada could not be neutral if Great Britain were at war, for Canada had not taken the additional legal steps which Eire and South Africa had taken to make this right clear. But while these constitutional ties remain it is well understood within the Commonwealth that they can be got rid of whenever the Dominion wants to get rid of them; their retention is voluntary and not compulsory. And it seems that Canada's separate declaration of war on September 10, 1939, one week after the British declaration, and the recognition by President Roosevelt of Canadian neutrality during that week of September 3–10, constitute adequate notice that in the future Canada is not committed to war save by her own act. The point is of some importance to Americans for this reason, that if they have guaranteed the defense of Canada, they naturally wish to know whether she is free to make peace and war through her own government alone or whether she can be brought into a war, and hence possibly involve joint defense measures, through the action of another government. Today the Canadian participation in wars in which Great Britain is engaged seems to have reached the point of being a matter of policy rather than a matter of legality. Eire has shown that the whole British Commonwealth does not have to be at war at the same time.

Canadian national feeling is more than a set of recent constitutional changes. These only reflect a growing sentiment of national unity and national responsibility: a natural desire on the part of 12,000,000 people to be as fully masters of their own destiny as any other people. Through the growth of this sentiment a closer cooperation between the French and British racial stocks, and indeed all other groups, has become possible, for all are Canadians. Canada's racial differences, while not to be overlooked or obliterated, take their place in the united nation as derivatives from the past rather than as directives for the future. As has been said, the division between nationalist and imperialist sentiment no longer runs on strictly racial lines in Canada. The statement of Lord Tweedsmuir, the Canadian Governor-General, in 1937, that "A Canadian's first loyalty is not to the British Commonwealth of Nations, but to Canada and to Canada's King", is a formula on which all races can meet.

The rise of Canadian nationalism has greatly improved Canadian-American relations. So long as the United States and Great Britain regarded Canada as a sort of "no-man's land" for the feud between them, all three countries had a hard time getting along. "The best thing that ever happened for friendly relations between all three parties", says Professor Chester Martin, "was the growth of deliberate, self-conscious, indigenous Canadian nationhood." [1]

Such, then, are the most important factors underlying the day-to-day conduct of Canadian-American affairs. Their amplification would take us beyond the limits of so short a survey. More has been said of Canadian than of American conditions, for the reason that Canadians, being a small population next a very great one, know far more about their neighbor than she knows about them. The need, therefore, is for more explanation from the Canadian side. With these factors before us, we may now proceed to examine some of the principal matters of controversy that have had to be settled by the two governments, the solution of which forms the main content of Canadian-American relations in the past. This will explain the present position into which the Ogdensburg Agreement must be fitted.

[1] *Conference on Canadian-American Affairs, 1935. Proceedings*, p. 154.

## 5. CHIEF DEVELOPMENTS IN CANADIAN-AMERICAN RELATIONS

### Boundaries

The first important matter which Canadians and Americans had to decide, once the American colonists had become a separate nation, was in what part of the continent each was to live. This took over a century to determine. The Treaty of Paris of 1783 settled the general position of the frontier, but not its exact location in some parts and not all the way across the continent. The boundary disputes which followed came after the migrations of the settlers, who pushed ever further west into the open country. So the first boundary arbitrations began in the East, to define the Maine-New Brunswick line. This came in three stages: the St. Croix River settlement in 1798, the Passamaquoddy Islands decision in 1817, and the final fixing of the northern Maine frontier in 1842. Thus was drawn the present rather irregular boundary in the East, which, though reasonable enough on the agreed grounds of decision, is so inconvenient for Canada that the main line of the Canadian Pacific Railway runs across American territory between Montreal and the Maritime Provinces. The Ashburton-Webster treaty of 1842 also drew the frontier through the Great Lakes and west along the 49th parallel. Then the Oregon territory and the Pacific coast were divided by the treaty of 1846—the

37

occasion of the "fifty-four forty or fight" cry. The line through the straits of Juan de Fuca was settled in 1872. In 1903 came the Alaskan award, the latest of these arbitrations, defining the westernmost limits of the now 5,500-mile boundary. More exact marking and monumentation of boundary lines was provided for by treaties of 1908 and 1925. The work is not yet complete.

Looking back over this long process of staking territorial claims, what is remarkable is that all the disputes were settled amicably by arbitration. The decisions were not always welcome. The Canadians were particularly concerned over the Maine and Alaskan awards, both of which isolate portions of Canadian territory, though the feeling here was as much directed against the British negotiators as against the United States. But through these experiences a practice and tradition of arbitration have grown up, which have been an outstanding characteristic of Canadian-American relations in the handling of all disputes which could not be settled by ordinary diplomatic methods, or by joint administrative boards.

It must not be imagined, however, that all the North American boundary questions are now safely out of the way. The political line is only one aspect of the boundary. Even this is not beyond alteration. In the far north of Alaska it may still be open to question. Canada lost a large piece of territory to Newfoundland in the Privy Council award of 1927 defining the "coast" of Labrador; and the future of Newfoundland is still obscure. Actually, some of the most important boundary problems occur around such things as the movement of settlers and visitors, the flow of goods, exchange rates, and now joint defense. Here a whole new group of questions has emerged, which may ultimately affect the political boundary.

Until very recently the Canadian-American boundary was no obstacle to people who wanted to move from one country to another. The story of the settling of North America shows a constant flow of population across the boundary both ways, in response to political and economic pressures. Settlers paid little attention to political sovereignty—except the Loyalists, and not all of them left the United States by preference. Yankees moved into Nova Scotia before the Revolution, Loyalists settled New Brunswick and Ontario, Britishers pushed into the American west, French Canadians filtered down into New England, Americans came up into the Canadian prairies. Thousands of Canadians in Windsor, Ontario, find their employment across the river in Detroit. American branch plants in Canada bring in personnel, American tourists visit the Dominion in large numbers. It has been estimated that some 30,000,000 crossings of the boundary were made in the year 1931. Thus has occurred that widespread mingling of the two peoples which gives so many Canadians and Americans relatives and friends in each other's country. Now with the war a great many new obstacles to this easy passage have arisen. The United States for the first time since the Civil War has insisted on passports for Canadians; and the Canadian government, in order to conserve exchange, will not allow Canadians to travel in the United States without a permit, which is never given for pleasure purposes. Americans do not need a passport to enter Canada, but to re-enter their own country they must establish their nationality. The movement of capital across the boundary is now strictly controlled. The sum total of these restrictions, to which both governments have contributed, means that a formidable social and financial boundary has now been added to the political one.

While this balkanizing process has been going on, the Ogdensburg defense agreement of August 1940 begins to expose its dangers. If troops should ever have to be moved across the frontier, they will not be asked for passports. American planes being delivered to Canada in the first months of the war used to be towed across the boundary instead of continuing their flight over it, in order to comply with American law; a touching tribute to legalism and sovereignty. Military highways will probably be needed to connect strategic points, regardless of the frontier. A proposal is already under consideration for a road through British Columbia which would give the United States a secure land route to Alaska. Out of the present situation many new boundary questions can be seen emerging.

## Boundary Waters

Where the Canadian-American boundary runs through rivers and lakes—which it does for about 1,800 miles—special problems arise. Navigation must be kept open. Dams may have to be built and electric power developed. Pollution by cities or industries must be controlled. Water levels must be maintained, for the drainage into the Great Lakes and St. Lawrence system can be deflected by man, and all shipping can be seriously affected by reducing the water-supply. In this field of Canadian-American relations, as with the political boundary, there has been a high degree of cooperation and a common-sense approach. The Boundary Waters treaty of 1909 between the United States and Great Britain (this was before Canada's treaty-making power was complete) provides the basis for this cooperation. The official body which settles all such questions as they arise is the International Joint Commission, consisting of three Americans and three Canadians appointed by their respective governments. No problem has yet developed which this Commission has been unable to deal with effectively. It is a permanent body, like the new Defense Board. Moreover its functions, besides including boundary waters questions over which its jurisdiction is compulsory, include also the settlement of any other disputes which Washington and Ottawa care to refer to it.

By various treaties the St. Lawrence, the Great Lakes including Lake Michigan, and other boundary waters are open to navigation on equal terms to all American and British subjects and vessels. The right also extends to all canals now built and to be built. Thus for navigation purposes there is no boundary along these waterways as between the United States and the British Commonwealth. Ships registered in any part of either may enjoy the natural advantages created by geography and improved by man along the Canadian-American frontier.

Further developments are being contemplated in the St. Lawrence system. The existing canals and locks enable ships of medium draught to pass from Montreal through to the head of Lake Superior. By enlarging these canals it would be possible to bring ocean-going vessels through the same route, so that no transhipment of cargoes would be necessary at any point. Duluth and other lake cities would then have direct water contact with the markets of the world. With the improvement in navigation would take place a great development of electric power, which could be shared by communities on both sides of the border. The scheme is grandiose in conception, and has been pushed with great vigor by various groups and individuals—including President Roosevelt—in recent years. In 1932 a treaty covering the proposal was concluded be-

41

tween Washington and Ottawa, but was rejected by the American Senate in 1933. Now the need for new electric power for defense purposes has revived the project, and negotiations between the two governments are continuing. The power aspects of the development appear more immediately realizable than the deep-navigation proposals, but the two cannot be altogether separated. There are many opponents as well as advocates of the idea, and it is still not clear what action will be taken.

## TARIFFS AND TRADE POLICY

Something has already been said of the close commercial relations between the United States and Canada, and of the considerable importance of Canada to American exporters and investors. Canadian dependence on the United States is naturally much greater. American trade policy, if suddenly altered, can inflict great damage on the Canadian economy. There have been several occasions— such as the ending of Reciprocity in 1866 and the enactment of the Smoot-Hawley tariff in 1930—when sudden changes have occurred. Canadians have always been a little wary of too great a dependence on American markets lest American policy should once more reverse itself and leave them dangerously stranded.

The history of Canadian-American trade relations has been a chequered one, showing at one moment a trend to reciprocity, at another a revival of protectionism. When Great Britain adopted free trade in the 1840's, Canada was suddenly deprived of her favored position in the old colonial empire. At once Canadian merchants turned to the United States for salvation. An important group of them in Montreal, seeing their incomes declining, even proposed that Canada be annexed to the United States,

42

and published a Manifesto (1849) calling for union of the two countries. Then in 1854 the situation was relieved by the first Reciprocity Treaty. Under this new régime prosperity returned to the British provinces. In 1866, however, the Reciprocity Treaty was cancelled by Washington, largely owing to resentment at British sympathies for the South during the Civil War. Canadians were once again thrown on their own resources, and there was no Imperial economic system to which they could turn. This time salvation was found in the political union of all the British North American provinces. The movement which, in 1867, created the present Dominion of Canada, received a powerful impetus from the ending of Reciprocity. Canadian business men hoped that, among other benefits from federal union, they would be able to build a strong commercial system of their own within the large free trade area which the union of 1867 established. American traders had grown rich exploiting the resources of their huge domain: why could not Canadians prosper likewise in their half of the continent? So Canada moved toward union of provinces and protection of home manufactures as her national policy.

Hence there has occurred, over a long period of time, the extensive development of railways and manufacturing plant on the Canadian side of the border. Today, as has been shown, Canada produces large surpluses in many commodities, which she exports to American and world markets. No doubt much of this industrial growth would have taken place under any trade policy, but a number of Canadian industries are children of the tariff and cannot exist without it. "The residue of industries brought into existence by the tariff and showing no appreciable progress toward independence of further tariff support has been

43

relatively much greater in Canada than in the United States, and in this sense the Canadian economic structure is a much more distorted one than the American."[1] In building this national economic system Canadians did not escape from American influence, for American capital was extensively used to finance the enterprise. The Canadian tariff, indeed, has been a major cause of the Americanization of Canadian industry for it has brought the American branch plant into Canada.

Despite the traditional national policy of Canada, a desire to increase the north-south flow of trade keeps coming to the fore in Canadian politics. Canada made many attempts to obtain a new reciprocity treaty after 1866, but met with continual rebuffs from Washington. In 1897 she adopted Imperial preference, and began to lean more strongly toward ideas of Empire trade. The longer the tariff barriers remained, the more difficult it became to increase the United States trade without injuring vested interests. When in 1911 President Taft and Sir Wilfrid Laurier concluded the second Reciprocity Treaty it was rejected by the Canadian people in a general election, largely because of a belief, strongly supported by business groups who feared lower tariffs, that closer economic ties would lead to annexation. The Fordney-McCumber and Smoot-Hawley tariffs of 1922 and 1930 cut off Canadian access to American markets more than ever. Then Canadians retaliated with large tariff increases in 1930, and in 1932 at Ottawa agreements were signed which attempted to make the whole British Commonwealth more self-sufficient. Incidentally Canadians hoped they would put pressure on the United States to make her relax her extreme protectionism.

[2] Dr. Jacob Viner, in *Proceedings*, 1935, *op. cit.*, p. 29.

So the trade relations of the two countries have wavered between opposing theories. Ideas of independence and national sovereignty have been uppermost. There was no joint policy being worked out, no attempt at long-range or continental planning. A change of party in one country generally meant a variation in the tariff, without, however, basically altering the continuing interrelationship of the two economies.

Shortly after the Ottawa Agreements, a change toward closer cooperation began. Mr. Roosevelt's "good neighbor" policy, Mr. Hull's program of reciprocal trade agreements, the loosening of traditional ideas brought about by the severity of the world depression, all made easier the path to freer exchange. When the new Trade Agreement of 1935 was announced it was received with universal approval in Canada; nobody raised the annexation cry as in 1911. Economic depression had been too deeply felt, and Canadians had lost most of their colonial mentality. The extension of the agreement in 1938 was similarly approved—this time for the added reason that it was accompanied by a British-American agreement. Today, though special problems have arisen on account of the war, Canadian-American trade relations are happier than they have been for a very long time. People are beginning to ask, Why not a Permanent Joint Economic Board along with the Joint Defense Board? "Ideally, of course, we should try to plan our tariff adjustments with the future goal of a rationalized economy on the North American continent."[1]

The actual extent of Canadian-American trade in 1938 by commodity groups is shown in the following table:

[2] Mr. Alex Skelton, in *Proceedings*, 1935, *op cit.*, p. 49.

## Canadian-United States Trade by Commodity Groups, 1938 [1]

### (In thousands of American dollars)

| Commodity Group | U. S. Exports to Canada (including reexports) | U. S. Imports from Canada (imports for consumption) |
|---|---|---|
| Animals and animal products, edible................ | $ 2,383 | $ 19,573 |
| Animals and animal products, inedible................ | 6,846 | 10,755 |
| Vegetable food products and beverages................ | 72,485 | 18,806 |
| Vegetable products, inedible, except fibers and wood........ | 10,096 | 2,106 |
| Textile fibers and manufactures. | 22,890 | 1,732 |
| Wood and paper............. | 14,559 | 145,357 |
| Nonmetallic minerals......... | 114,583 | 11,456 |
| Metals and manufactures, except machinery and vehicles...... | 39,372 | 21,195 |
| Machinery and vehicles....... | 118,379 | 2,722 |
| Chemicals and related products. | 22,292 | 10,520 |
| Miscellaneous domestic articles, including total reexports of foreign merchandise........ | 43,882 | 12,425 |
| Total................. | $467,767 | $256,647 |

## Fisheries

The Newfoundland and North Atlantic Fisheries were among the earliest of the resources in North America to be exploited by Europeans. French and, later, British sailors developed a thriving trade in codfish which they caught on the Grand Banks and in the Gulf of St. Lawrence, and sold in home markets. As settlement along the

[1] *Trade of the United States with Canada in* 1938, U. S. Department of Commerce. Issued by Division of Business Review, May 1939.

Atlantic coast developed the colonists themselves became the principal fishermen. International struggles over the fisheries gradually changed from being primarily Franco-British to being British-American and now Canadian-American. The diplomatic history has been long and the relations often strained. At various times rights have been defined by treaty; then existing treaties have proven inadequate to meet changed conditions and new agreements have been made. There have been a number of arbitrations of particular disputes, the most important being the North Atlantic Fisheries Arbitration of 1910. Under this award a Permanent Mixed Fishery Commission was proposed for Canada and the United States, to deal with certain fishery questions in the future. This procedure was accepted by an Agreement of 1912. Here again is an example of a growing tendency to refer matters of importance to the United States and Canada, after a long experience with *ad hoc* treaties and arbitrations, to a special body of experts.

The history of fisheries agreements in the North Atlantic has its parallel in the North Pacific area. Here the chief industries have been the catch of fur-bearing seal, of halibut and of the sockeye salmon. Outstanding differences between Canada and the United States regarding the seal catch were settled by the Behring Sea Arbitration Award of 1893. In 1911 the United States, Great Britain (for Canada), Russia and Japan, all of whom were interested, agreed to prohibit the killing of seals in the seas north of the 30th parallel of latitude. Recently (1940) Japan has given notice of her intention to terminate this treaty on the ground that seals have increased so much they threaten the fishing industry of the area; thus the question of seal killing is again open, with the United

States and Canada both interested. In 1923 Ottawa and Washington negotiated a treaty governing the taking of halibut in the North Pacific; this was the occasion when Canada first successfully claimed the right to make her own treaties in the name of His Majesty without the assistance of a British representative. Under this Halibut Treaty, now replaced by the later agreement of 1937, an International Fisheries Commission was set up to propose regulations for preserving the halibut industry. A similar convention in 1930 appointed another International Commission to regulate the sockeye salmon catch in the Fraser River system.

Canada and the United States are interested in another common fishing ground—the Great Lakes. Recently it was found necessary to make joint plans for protecting this industry also. Thus out of the economic exploitation of boundary and adjacent waters the Canadian and American people have learned to work together, and have evolved sensible techniques for dealing with common problems. The permanent joint board has become a standard device. The arbitration of the nineteenth century seems to be developing into joint administration in the twentieth.

## Communications

People in the United States and Canada have such frequent need to communicate with one another, to travel, trade and talk across the frontier, that it is not surprising to find a host of agreements of one sort and another relating to communications. The right of free and equal navigation, it has been pointed out, was early guaranteed along boundary and neighboring waters. Shipping communication is thus made easy, though each country regulates its own coastal trade. The railway systems of the two countries are closely interrelated. From the earliest days Canadian railways have crossed the frontier. The old Grand Trunk line ran west from Canada to Chicago, and had its eastern outlet at Portland, Maine. The Canadian Pacific Railway's eastern line to St. John, New Brunswick, cuts across Maine, and the C.P.R. also owns important lines south of the Great Lakes, linking its eastern and western divisions through American territory. American railroads have lines and trackage rights in Canada. "In their penetration of the country across the border the rail carriers of Canada, as of 1933, have acquired control or exercise trackage rights over 7312 miles of road in the United States, and, conversely, the American carriers possess similar privileges over 1556 miles of road in Canada".[1] There are some fifty railroad "gateways" across the boundary. In the United States the Interstate Commerce Commission, and in Canada the Board of Transport Commissioners, exercise government regulation over rates and other matters; these agencies work in close cooperation. In line with developments in other fields, an International Commerce Commission for the two countries was actually proposed and a draft treaty drawn up in 1911 to establish it; but the idea was dropped at the time and has not since been revived.[2]

The radio creates a new link between the two countries. In the United States broadcasting is carried on by private companies operating under federal license. Canada has adopted the British system of government operation under a public body, the Canadian Broadcasting Corporation.

[1] Wilgus, A. Curtis, *The Railway Interrelations of the United States and Canada*, p. 21.
[2] The text of the treaty is in Wilgus, *op. cit.*, p. 249.

This means more complete state control in Canada than in the United States though many licensed private stations still are allowed to operate north of the border. For obvious reasons Canadians hear American programs much more than Americans hear Canadian ones, and the radio is undoubtedly extending American influence and ideas in Canada. It should not be supposed, however, that the effect of the radio is to weaken national sentiment in Canada, for now Canadians have a mechanism which overcomes some of the obstacles to unity arising from the enormous size of the country, and through which one voice can speak to the whole nation at the same time. The Canadian Broadcasting Corporation has followed a balanced policy of linking up with the American chains for the more important and more popular features, and at the same time developing a number of purely Canadian programs of an educational, artistic, historical and patriotic kind. French-Canadian programs now also reach down to the French Canadians in New England, reviving the sense of a "motherland" among immigrants of more recent years. Radio's influence in bringing all parts of Canada together is probably more important than its influence in making American programs available. The use of the air, however, requires close cooperation between Washington and Ottawa as regards wave-lengths and network facilities. The United States and Canada are bound, with other countries, by the International Telecommunication Convention of 1932.

The great development of air transport in recent years opens up similar possibilities of intercommunication and presents further need for cooperation. Here again are found special arrangements embodied in treaties. On December 11, 1940, a new agreement was announced providing for reciprocal treatment in the operation of air services between the two countries, and including provision for aids to air navigation along the coast of British Columbia. The Associated Press on January 12, 1941, reported that Ottawa was planning a string of airbases from Edmonton across northern Alberta, northern British Columbia and the Yukon to Alaska, and attributed the plan to the Joint Defense Board. This would give a year-round direct air route from Alaska to the United States.

Much could be said of the intellectual cooperation and communication between the United States and Canada. It is enough here to note its existence and to stress its importance, particularly in the life of Canada. The exchanges of university teachers and students, the international character of the A.F. of L. and C.I.O. trades unions, the visits of friends and business acquaintances, the flow of books, magazines, moving pictures and radio programs, all account for a growing intercommunication of ideas. Unofficial agencies have come into being to promote better understanding and to provide opportunities for more advanced discussion of common problems. The Canadian Institute of International Affairs cooperates with such groups as the Institute of Pacific Relations, the Foreign Policy Association, the Council on Foreign Relations and the World Peace Foundation. The Carnegie Endowment for International Peace has organized special conferences on Canadian-American Affairs in 1935, 1937 and 1939, the proceedings of which have been published. The same Endowment has also sponsored a series of authoritative studies on the relations of the United States and Canada, in whose volumes (fifteen already published, and more to come) can be found fuller information about many subjects touched upon in this pamphlet.

For about a century after the American War of Independence Canadians were thinking of defense mainly in terms of defense against the United States. Twice invading armies of Americans had to be prevented from conquering the country; the Oregon boundary question brought President Polk into office on the cry "Fifty-four forty or fight"; the Civil War brought tensions which might have led to war and did lead to the Fenian raids. Canadian federal union in 1867 was desired in part as a means of strengthening the defense forces in Canada. From the American point of view northern expansion appealed both as "manifest destiny" and as defense against British power. After 1870 the British withdrew their troops from Canada except for small garrisons at Halifax and Esquimault (withdrawn in 1905), and Canadians thenceforth assumed responsibility for their own local defense. Since then there has been little if any military fear in Canada of attack from the United States, and Canadian defense policy does not take such a contingency into account.

Even in the midst of the early period, however, cooperation on defense questions began. The Rush-Bagot agreement of 1817, by which the Great Lakes and Lake Champlain were limited as to naval vessels, marked the first step toward joint military action. This was a disarmament move; it laid the basis for the tradition of the "undefended frontier". The Monroe Doctrine, though enunciated primarily with a view to Central and South America, implied also a protection of Canada if she were threatened with invasion. The seeds of the continental idea were thus planted early, but conditions had to change before they were to bring forth fruit. Now conditions have changed, rapidly and radically. Canada fully controls her own defense policy and is no longer just an "outpost" of Britain. Britain herself is no longer a threat to America, but a buffer state against new threats. A common danger confronts the United States and Canada, and defense becomes a matter, not of protection against each other, but of mutual security against the outside world.

It was in 1938 that President Roosevelt made explicit the implied defense guarantee of the Monroe Doctrine. Speaking at Queen's University in Kingston, Ontario, on August 18, he said: "The Dominion of Canada is part of the sisterhood of the British Empire. I give you assurance that the people of the United States will not stand idly by if domination of Canadian soil is threatened by any other empire." Mr. King acknowledged the offer with becoming gratitude, though disclaiming then any idea of a military alliance. The incident could hardly have been casual or unpremeditated, for conversations relating to joint defense, we now know, had begun the year before. Coming as a unilateral declaration, the President's statement prepared the ground for the next move, at Ogdensburg, New York. There, on August 17, 1940, during military manoeuvres which Mr. Roosevelt had invited Mr. King to attend, the leaders of the two democratic states announced the conclusion of the defense agreement in these words:

> The Prime Minister and the President have discussed the mutual problems of defense in relation to the safety of Canada and the United States.
> It has been agreed that a Permanent Joint Board on Defense shall be set up at once by the two countries.
> This Permanent Joint Board on Defense shall commence

immediate studies relating to sea, land and air problems including personnel and material.

It will consider in the broad sense the defense of the north half of the Western Hemisphere.

The Permanent Joint Board on Defense will consist of four or five members from each country, most of them from the services. It will meet shortly.

Five days after the agreement was announced, the new Permanent Joint Board was appointed. The Hon. Fiorello H. La Guardia was named head of the United States Section, and Col. O. M. Biggar, K. C., of the Canadian Section. The other members of the Joint Board include representatives of each of the army, navy and air services of the two countries, and a secretary for each of the Sections from the Department of State and the Department of External Affairs respectively.

Thus to the other subjects such as Boundaries, Waterways, Trade Agreements, Fisheries and Communications, which have formed the principal topics of "Canadian-American relations" in the past, must now be added that of the Defense Agreement. To the permanent boards already in existence to deal with questions of boundary waters, Atlantic fisheries and Pacific fisheries, must be added the new Permanent Joint Board on Defense. Between Canada and the United States the administrative machinery for cooperation on a large scale is steadily growing.

## 6. *WHAT DOES OGDENSBURG MEAN?*

In area Canada is half the North American continent. She commands the entrance to the only great waterway leading into the interior from the east coast. She guards the doors to the northern frontier of the United States. When the United States and Canada plan defense jointly, North America becomes a single huge island, and strategy can be the strategy of defending an island. When they act separately, the island is partitioned. Through joint action Alaska ceases to be isolated from the rest of United States territory, and naval bases in New England, Nova Scotia and Newfoundland can be integrated with the common plan. Hitherto Alaska, the portion of North America nearest Asia, and Newfoundland, the portion nearest Europe, have been politically cut off from their adjoining territory.

Industrially Canada is among the leading world powers. She has great resources of raw materials, a large and expanding industrial plant. She built a powerful war machine during the years 1914–1918, and is doing so again. Her war potential is greater than that of any other nation in the Western Hemisphere except the United States. Through Canadian-American cooperation, a total population of 143,000,000 people, controlling the economic resources of the world's greatest and the world's sixth largest trading nation, can organize for defense over 6,000,000 square miles of contiguous land, bounded by three oceans and a narrow isthmus.

Americans have generally thought of Latin America first when discussing hemisphere defense. Ogdensburg symbolizes the recognition of the great importance of Canada in this whole picture. The Canadian-American joint defense board is the first permanent board of its kind to be set up between any American nations.

Though Canada has only a small population in a huge territory, it is important to realize that she can prepare and is preparing defenses that would be very effective against any attempt at invasion. There are few points where attack upon her would be possible for an overseas power. The Pacific coast is rugged, difficult to navigate, and backed by high mountains. It lends itself to coastal defense, which is being steadily augmented. Hudson Bay might be entered by aircraft carriers whose planes could conceivably bomb cities in central Canada, some 500 miles away; but the Bay is open to navigation for about two months only in the year, and defending planes, using home bases, could deal with any forces that might risk the attempt. On the east lie the St. Lawrence gateway and the Maritime Provinces. The St. Lawrence is closed by ice five months of the year, and can be easily mined. The control of the Gulf and defense of the Maritime Provinces present a more serious problem, yet even here Canadians have felt that their coastal, air and naval forces can provide defenses so strong that no enemy would care to attack until he had at least achieved complete mastery of the North Atlantic. In short, Canadians can and are looking after their home defenses, with their own resources of men and materials. "Canadian achievements and preparations, in army, air force and war industry, have provided the United States with an unexpectedly effective defense of her supposedly undefended long northern boundary." [1]

What Canada cannot undertake is anything like command of the high seas off her coasts, or even the holding of those islands which constitute the outer ring of North American defenses, like Greenland, Iceland and the West Indies. These larger schemes involve capital ships and heavy naval units which Canadians cannot build and which their economy could not maintain in sufficient quantity. Newfoundland, because closer to Canada, is more within her sphere of action; Canadian troops have been placed there, and talk of its incorporation in the Dominion (it is now, with Labrador, a British colony governed direct from London) is being revived; but the United States has obtained a naval base there already, for she cannot wait until Canada might be ready to assume responsibility. No small power can ever match the great powers in shipbuilding, or hope to be able to protect its merchant shipping all round the world. Canada's contribution to North American defense lies in her ability to defend her own coasts, to provide certain valuable war materials, and in her willingness to co-ordinate her defense plans with the continental and hemispheric needs of the United States.

It would therefore be wrong to suppose that in coming to Ogdensburg to negotiate the defense agreement Mr. King was representing a frightened and helpless small power running for assistance to a big neighbor. The facts suggest otherwise. The talks that culminated in the pub-

---

[1] Brebner, J. Bartlet in "Ogdensburg: A Turn in Canadian-American Relations," *Inter-American Quarterly*, October 1940.

lished agreement began, Mr. King told the Canadian House of Commons, in 1937, before the European situation was anything like as menacing as it has since become. Canada's war effort, by August 1940, was well advanced.[1] The fall of France and other German successes made the timing of the agreement most opportune for political purposes in both countries, but something of the sort would almost certainly have come into the open sooner or later. Canada too was acting as a "good neighbor" in the situation, being anxious to cooperate with the United States so as to produce the maximum security in North America with the minimum of effort and expense. There is common sense in such an arrangement at any time.

## THE NATURE OF THE AGREEMENT

No formal treaty was concluded at Ogdensburg. The agreement was merely an understanding between the heads of two governments. There was no exchange of diplomatic notes of any kind, incorporating the published terms of the agreement, as in the destroyer-bases deal. Ogdensburg did not rest upon sanction by the United States Senate, nor does it bind His Majesty on behalf of Canada. Technically it is liable to termination at any time by either party. Its essence is in the agreement to collaborate on problems of joint defense. As Colonel Biggar, Chairman of the Canadian section of the Joint Board, expressed it, "The setting up of the Board imposes no obligation on either country. The Board's function is to study the problems which arise and to report from time to time to the two governments the steps it thinks should be taken."

[1] For surveys of Canada's war effort and production see, *Fortune*, November 1940; *Foreign Affairs*, October 1940 and January 1941.

The terms of Ogdensburg are very general. There is no agreement to render military aid in specific circumstances; no formalization of the President's promise at Queen's University. The only thing agreed to is that a permanent joint board will be set up, and that it will "study" questions of defense. The Board has no executive power; only if its reports are accepted by the two governments does further joint action occur. Moreover, the reports, being defense matters, will not be published. But the implication of joint action is clear enough. Though strictly speaking Ogdensburg is not a treaty of defensive alliance, when taken in conjunction with the Monroe Doctrine, President Roosevelt's promise at Queen's University, and the fact that the defense board is permanent, it approaches the same thing. In the statement already quoted, Colonel Biggar used these words:

> You cannot solve suddenly problems of common defense. All the possible dangers from enemy operations must be the subject of profound study in advance of common action. The governments of the two countries concerned must reach agreement as to the responsibilities each is to assume. These responsibilities must be carefully defined. Each government must be satisfied that the other is capable of carrying out the task allotted to it. There must be an understanding about the way the forces of each are to be reinforced by those of the other. Troop movements must be co-ordinated; the capacity of the available transportation facilities taken into account; methods of communication between the forces of each country arranged, and points with regard to supply and the like worked out in detail. In addition to all this you have to provide for elasticity in the plans.

Ogdensburg may not have been surrounded with the technicalities of diplomacy, but it rests on the more solid ground of geography and military necessity, and community of interests.

The agreement was more of an innovation for Canada than for the United States. Ogdensburg fits easily into the Pan American policy of Mr. Roosevelt, just as does the destroyer-bases deal. For America the novelty lay in the sudden realization that Canada, for geographic and economic reasons, plays a vital role in hemisphere preparedness. Canada, on the other hand, has had no continental defense policy at all: quite the reverse. Ogdensburg is thus a new departure for Canadians. It means that they have at last appreciated the strategic requirements of their North American position. It means that Ottawa has faced the military facts of the modern world, its new techniques of warfare and its changing balances of power, and has begun to make Canadian territory secure by cooperation with the nearest great power which can defend her. It is an acknowledgment that, no matter how important it may be to meet the enemy in other places before he reaches your shore, sound public policy and plain common sense require that home defense and strategy should be adapted to the new realities of danger from East and West.

No Canadian Government that took its duties seriously could do otherwise. Home defense must take precedence over external action even though the two are related. Mr. Mackenzie King has explained his attitude in these words: "All through the days and months which have passed since war was declared the government has held to that one position, that we were fighting at the side of Britain against aggression; and in doing so we have noted particularly two obligations: one, the primary obligation of defense of our country; second, cooperation with our forces at the side of Britain in Britain herself." [Speech of November 12, 1940.] A few years ago Ottawa began a general strengthening of Canada's coastal defenses, and Ogdensburg is a logical outcome of such plans. But never before have Canadians thought of defense in these continental terms.

Because Canada is already at war, with her military production and training planned for assistance to Britain in Europe, the acceptance of additional responsibility for home defense necessitates some division of war effort as between overseas and North American requirements. This is both natural and inevitable. Every strategist has to face a similar problem who keeps his second line of defense ready while supporting the first line. Britain had to be ready to hold the Channel after she fell back from the Rhine. Canada till now has had no effective North American line of defense; she has always concentrated her attention, at least during this century, on overseas war. There are still people in Canada who adopt a defeatist attitude when the idea of defending Canada in North America is mentioned, and who feel it is being disloyal to suggest that if Britain is lost all is not lost. It has seemed almost treasonable, as Professor Brebner notes, to give much thought to an arrangement like Ogdensburg, the importance of which would increase with every loss in British power and effectiveness. The effect of the fall of France, however, was to bring home the need for continental defense at the same time as it increased the desire to aid overseas.

Even so, there is a real difference for Canada between certain types of equipment needed for overseas and for home defense. For troops cooperating with the British forces in Europe, British models and specifications are desirable; for troops prepared and equipped to fight in

North America, co-ordination with American standards and types is needed. The Canadian portion of North American defense cannot depend upon British supplies; it must be continentally self-contained. Once already in this war, after the collapse of France, Canadian defense plans have had to be changed because the British needed at home the training equipment they had promised to Canada. For home defense Canadian troops must learn how to manoeuvre with modern equipment in the Canadian climate. Thus Canadians must work out two separate, though to some degree overlapping, plans of campaign—a tidy problem for a country of twelve million. The United States also finds she must apportion her defense efforts as between North American and hemisphere defense, and aid to Britain.

## Aid to Britain

Is Ogdensburg really a North American pact, or is it primarily designed to aid Britain? The question has been more debated in Canada than in the United States. Those Canadians who tend to think of British needs first hope that Ogdensburg will mean greater American aid to Britain, or are fearful it may detract from the overseas effort. Others who think first of Canada emphasize that it is what it purports to be—a plan for the joint defense of this continent. The usual dualism in Canadian thinking can be seen here. Most people, however, see that it serves the two purposes of defending Canada and at the same time making possible closer Canadian-American co-operation.

Senator Meighen, an ardent Imperialist, said in the Canadian Senate on November 13, 1940: "All this inspecting of aerodromes and harbors on the Atlantic coast and the putting of some guns on the Pacific, and Mr. La Guardia's speeches, I do not know how to describe, but I do know the effect is to induce our people to hide and seek refuge under a delusion, to turn their eyes from unpleasant and forbidding truths. Of what value would these local defenses be if the British fleet should lose control of the Atlantic?" The answer is, of course, that they would not only be valuable in such an unfortunate eventuality, but would be critically important, as everyone would immediately recognize. Perhaps to meet this kind of attack, Mr. King, explaining the agreement to the Canadian Parliament on November 12, 1940, took pains to show how strongly it was approved by English opinion. He referred to the very special role which Canada had to play "in the promotion of Anglo-American friendship", and quoted the comment on Ogdensburg by the London *Times*, which said: "The two countries will henceforward have closer ties than they have had in the past, and Canada more than ever before will be the linchpin of Anglo-American relations."

The terms of reference of the Joint Defense Board are to "consider in the broad sense the defense of the northern half of the Western Hemisphere." This means defending America, down to the Canal Zone, since the word "hemisphere" is used. But plans for defending half a hemisphere today cannot possibly ignore the actualities of the moment—and actually Canada and Britain are at war with one of the only two powers, Germany and Japan, which threaten this hemisphere. The enlargement of the scale of modern warfare, the long range of new fighting craft, and the world plans of opposing political systems, all compel defense experts to think in world terms to a greater degree than they have ever done before. The American public has shown its appreciation of this need by its recognition that aid to Britain operates as defense of America. Thus the contrast between "defending America" and "aiding Britain", though still a real contrast, is no longer as sharp as it formerly was. It is more a matter of emphasis and of priorities; of how much effort shall be spent, and where.

So long as Canada fights with Britain, everything which strengthens her position is indirectly an aid to Britain. If Canada did not plan her home defense in conjunction with the United States, she would have to do it by herself: this would obviously be more difficult and more costly, and hence would detract more from her overseas effort.

Ogdensburg is clearly not of itself a step taking the United States into the war or into alliance with the British Empire, even though it will increase the collaboration with the Empire. It simply rounds out the American policy of hemisphere consolidation. Similar to the joint defense plans with Canada are the military conversations and exchanges of information which have already taken place between the United States and the Latin American republics. Ogdensburg links Canada to the inter-American system.

Perhaps we may discern, underlying these surface negotiations, a more fundamental process at work. This is the expansion of our political concepts to keep pace with man's technical capacity for large-scale organization. Mass production, the industrialization of warfare, the perfection of the internal combustion engine, the science of planning—these basic factors have rendered obsolete the anarchic world of small national sovereignties in which we used to live. A supra-nationalism, a higher federalism, seems to be developing. Ogdensburg is but a straw in that historic wind, important though it is in itself. It is a step along the road of greater international collaboration which all nations are being compelled to travel.

As Mr. King said in the Canadian House of Commons:

> The link forged by the Canada-United States defense agreement is no temporary axis. It was not formed by nations whose common tie is a mutual desire for the destruction of their neighbors. It is part of the enduring foundation of a new world order, based on friendship and good will. In the furtherance of this new world order, Canada, in liaison between the British Commonwealth and the United States, is fulfilling a manifest destiny.

It is now the turn of a Canadian to use the term "manifest destiny", in a new and more democratic sense.

### Joint Defense Needs Joint Economic Planning

The defense agreement is bound to produce changes in the commercial relations of the two countries. Defense, as Colonel Biggar pointed out, involves questions of transportation, communication and supply. Joint defense, to be effective, means joint economic planning. There must be agreement as to which country is going to produce what armaments and in what quantity. Canada's war production, having had a longer start, is ahead of that of the United States in some respects. She is making very large quantities of ammunition, shells, small arms, and general supplies; as the center of the British Commonwealth Air Training Plan she is about to turn out large numbers of pilots and airmen. She can produce war material of many sorts, as she can produce the commodities of peaceful trade, far in excess of her own needs.

These factors are doubtless being considered by the Joint Board in laying plans for common action.

On the other hand, some types of war equipment cannot be produced by Canada at all, or only at great cost. This applies generally to the heavier types of material. Heavy guns, heavy tanks, heavy ships, flying fortresses—for their manufacture Canadian industry is not suited. Airplane engines also are outside her present range. A logical division of labor between the United States and Canada for defense purposes would allot to each country the types of military production in which its industry can most efficiently engage. "There is obviously a great deal of waste and duplication involved in the spectacle of two adjacent economies aiming at all-round defense production each in his own preserve and separated by artificial tariff barriers from each other. Both countries are conducting their production programs strictly on the principle of nationalism." [1]

At present the Canadian exchange problem makes such a division of labor very difficult. Canada buys more from the United States than she sells to her, and must husband her dollar resources. She is forced by this economic pressure to free herself as far as possible from further dependence on American imports. Something has already been said of the financial strain upon Canada owing to her unbalanced trade with the United States and to the impossibility of changing surplus pounds sterling into American dollars due to British exchange controls. The actual figures for the balance of payments are alarming to Canadians. They work out approximately as follows for the year 1940: [2]

[1] *Plan Age*, November-December 1940, p. 297.
[2] See Grant Dexter, *Foreign Affairs*, January 1941.

## Canadian Balance of Payments with the United States

### (In millions of Canadian dollars)

| Debits | | Credits | |
|---|---|---|---|
| Net Commodity trade...... | 300 | Net Tourist receipts.... | 150 |
| Interest and Dividends.... | 250 | Gold production.......... | 205 |
| Freight and Miscellaneous | 45 | | |
| Total......................... | 595 | Total.................... | 355 |

This leaves a debit balance of $245,000,000. For 1941 and 1942 the deficit will almost certainly be greater, for as Canada's war production expands her imports from the United States will increase faster than her exports. Such a deficit cannot continue indefinitely.

To meet the problem various steps may be taken. First, Canadians can stop purchasing "unessential" commodities from the United States—cars, radios, luxury goods and foodstuffs—and can reduce their travel in the United States to a minimum. Both of these steps have already been taken. Second, Canada may try to produce as much as possible of the war material now being imported; she may turn to military economic nationalism. This is also occurring. Production of heavy guns, heavy tanks and airplane engines is being planned, despite its economic wastefulness. Thirdly, Canada may liquidate her investments in the United States, as the British are doing. So far this has not been attempted, though the Canadian Foreign Exchange Control Board has compelled all Canadians to hand over their American cash holdings. Fourthly, Canada may try to increase her exports to the United States, both visible and invisible. Also, Canada could tax the interest and dividends paid in the United States.

These forms of economic action are likely to affect

Canadian-American trade relations very considerably. They also raise problems for the Joint Defense Board. If Canada reduces her American imports too far on non-military goods, she endangers the existing Trade Agreement, which no one wishes to see cancelled. The stopping of Canadian travel in the United States creates a real barrier between the two peoples just when they should be understanding one another better. In so far as Canada begins to make war equipment that the United States can produce more cheaply, a wastage of resources takes place which weakens the total North American position. The sale of Canadian investments in the United States would not be so effective as the figures at first suggest; though Canada's total investment is about $1,100,000,000, much of this is in properties (*e.g.* railroads) which cannot readily be sold. Portfolio investments probably do not exceed $500,000,000 in book value, perhaps $350,000,000 in market value. The sale of these securities, apart from the effect on the American security markets, would be only a temporary alleviation of the difficulty. Canada has hesitated to place special taxes on foreign interest payments, though these are a great strain on the exchange.

Probably the increase of Canadian exports to the United States is the most desirable solution from the Canadian point of view. This might occur in various ways. If twice as many American tourists could be induced to visit Canada in 1941 as went there in 1940, the situation would be noticeably eased. It has been suggested that the United States might pay for the construction of strategic airfields and harbors on the Atlantic and Pacific coasts of Canada; if the materials and labor were obtained in Canada, Canada's gain in U. S. dollars would be considerable. Another possibility would be such a well-knit policy of joint production and mutual use of resources that the exchange problem would iron itself out in a new system amounting largely to barter.[1] Such a solution would be both thorough and lasting. Again, it would help to equalize the trade if the United States would lower still further her tariff on Canadian goods. For though Canadians are no longer buying luxury articles from American manufacturers, their total purchases of American produce are higher than ever before. The customs barrier between the two countries begins to get in the way of joint defense.[2]

Another way of easing Canada's financial situation remains. The United States could amend the Neutrality Act and extend a loan to Canada. It would not be necessary to amend the Johnson Act also, for Canada paid back every cent of what she borrowed from the United States during the last war. Loans carry certain political implications, however, of deep concern to both the United States and Canada. If a loan were made, Washington might well wish to have some say as to how the money would be spent. Would there be a preference for a North American war effort rather than for a European war effort? Canadians might welcome financial aid, but scarcely if it were going to involve some loss of their political freedom.

Today Canadians find themselves in the curious position that the more they contribute toward an overseas war effort, the more they push themselves toward financial dependence on the United States. This happens in two ways. First, they must buy more and more supplies from

[1] See *Plan Age*, November-December 1940, *passim*.
[2] Discussion has already started as to whether the customs wall could be removed. See, for instance, an interesting article on the United States and Canada in *Plan Age*, September 1940.

the United States to maintain their war production; this leads to exchange difficulties, to a desire for wider markets in America, and to a need for American financial assistance. Second, the chief way in which Britain can pay Canada for war materials is by liquidating her Canadian investments; this tends to convert Canada from a debtor to a creditor nation *vis-a-vis* Britain, with the long-term result that Britain will not be able to buy so much from Canada in the future, and the British market will decline in relative importance. In an economic sense, therefore, Canadians become more American by being more strongly pro-British. If Canadians care for their separate existence as a nation, they cannot think only of military operations in Europe, but must think also of the economic results of such effort, particularly as regards their relations with the United States.

The economic aspects of joint defense are so important that the question arises whether some special agency is not needed to study them. The present Defense Board is primarily military. It has so far made but few reports and none public. It will require further assistance on the economic side as its studies develop. Canadians are deeply concerned in the working of the Priorities Board at Washington; its decisions affect the availability of supplies that Canada needs for her war production. A certain amount of United States steel is essential to Canadian defense plans, for instance, and American exporters must obtain a license before they can ship it abroad. The British are also interested in the distribution of American supplies, and as American policy is to aid Britain as well as to collaborate with Canada, a three-way division of effort seems desirable. "What is needed and needed quickly, before the economic life of the two countries [Canada and the United States] drifts further and further apart is a Canadian body of industrial economic and military experts, with full powers, to work in close collaboration with the British Purchasing Commission and to be continually on the spot to consult with and lay its ideas before the Defense Commission." [1] The placing of the Hon. C. D. Howe, Canadian Minister of Munitions and Supply, on the British Supply Council set up in January 1941, is a step in that direction.

## DEFENSE—OF WHAT?

Defense depends on policy. Something is being defended. What is it? Unless there be agreement on that, defense cannot be planned. If one country were aiming to promote fascism and the other democracy, joint defense would be impossible. A profoundly important implication of Ogdensburg is that both Canada and the United States are in agreement upon basic principles of national policy.

What are the elements of that common national policy? It seems that three underlying, North American principles can be distinguished.

The first is that North America shall not suffer military invasion and conquest. These are days when all eventualities must be fearlessly faced, and it is not safe to make assumptions as to "impossible" events or "unthinkable" circumstances. The United States and Canada are confronting a changing world. It must be faced boldly. The United States is the most powerful nation there is; North America as a continent is even more powerful. The peoples of the continent are united in their determination to remain free, and though fully realizing present dangers

[1] *Plan Age*, November-December 1940, p. 300.

are confident of success. If the plans for joint action are vigorously carried forward there is little need for defeatism in this part of the world, no matter what the future may hold in store.

The second element common to American and Canadian policy is the recognition of their joint interests in other parts of the globe. Whether this comes from an extension of the idea of continental defense, or from an altrustic desire to help victims of aggression abroad, is less important than the fact of mutual concern. Both countries have the same friends, and the same enemies, abroad. Opinions may differ as to the degree of assistance to be rendered in particular cases, but they do not differ as to who should receive help. Canada has gone to war to aid Britain, and in so far as Americans believe that aiding Britain is defending America, they must recognize that Canada is also defending America by her war effort. Canada, on the other hand, pays little attention to the Chinese war against aggression. The United States is increasing her aid to Britain, and also is giving direct assistance to China. The United States is playing a leading part in developing Pan American collaboration; Canada is beginning to realize how important this is to her also. The broad lines of international policy run parallel. Ogdensburg was concerned primarily with the military defense of North America, but underlying it is a world outlook shared by both peoples.

The third element is the most important of all, because it touches the realm of spirit and of faith. This is a common determination that the democratic way of life shall continue to develop in the world. This alone can give the joint defense efforts a high and lasting purpose. The original intent of settlers coming both to the United

States and to Canada was to create a new society embodying the best elements in their past tradition. Though much was imported that led to strife and oppression, the democratic idea has prevailed and has been enlarged. Today it provides a unifying purpose and goal. It is never-ending, leading from achievement to achievement. It is not only a desire for material prosperity and a mastery of nature, but for spiritual and intellectual freedom, for racial and religious toleration, for liberty of the person, for a sense of community and brotherhood—in short, for a full democracy. The United States and Canada have both travelled far along the democratic road, but both have much to do to complete their democracy, particularly in the economic sphere. The need today is not just to maintain the existing order, but for a new advance. If joint defense plans are to stir the imagination and to evoke the willing support of the common people of the continent, they must relate to a social idea that is vital and dynamic. Social maladjustment within can be as dangerous as a lack of armaments; unemployment, insecurity, poverty alongside of luxury, are subversive of the democratic order. The ideas of strengthening democracy at home and defending it abroad are not two, but one, and through collaboration on both fronts the United States and Canada will find their greatest contribution to humanity.

# 7. *THE FUTURE*

The world is in the throes of a great transition. The gravest issues are at stake in the present war. Yet if we narrow our view to the future relations of Canada and the United States, it seems likely that the growing cooperation between the two countries will continue in almost any eventuality.

If the Axis powers should dominate Europe, Asia and Africa, and should then seek to dominate the Americas, a common fear would drive the United States and Canada even closer together. The loose understanding of Ogdensburg would need replacing by a formal alliance, and Canada would be obliged to subordinate her foreign policy to that of Washington. This would not necessarily mean the annexation of Canada, any more than of Mexico, but it would mean integration of policies and much more joint military and economic planning. While some sentiment in favor of annexation is often to be found in Canada, and would be likely to increase under desperate threats from abroad, nevertheless the national consciousness among Canadians may be counted on to oppose total absorption by the United States even when it would welcome extensive cooperation. A small power may move in the orbit of a larger power without thereby losing its identity. Any union in the future is less likely to come through outright annexation than through joint merging in some supra-national organization.

74

On the other hand an Allied victory, on whatever terms it may come, can never exactly restore the former international relationships. Even if no world system is built, some new order will have to be formed in Europe in which Britain is likely to collaborate more closely with continental powers. The offer of union with France in 1940, which would have radically altered the Commonwealth structure if it had materialized, is perhaps a foretaste of what may come. The various parts of the Empire will almost certainly be more intimately associated with the peoples of their adjoining areas. Economic separateness of neighbors would be no better basis for peace in the future than it proved to be in the past. Regionalism seems to be on the increase, owing to technological and other influences, and this will make for closer Canadian-American cooperation.

If a new world order is to be built under the leadership of the democracies, Britain and the United States will have to be its mainstays. Germany will waste no time creating her new world order if given the opportunity; if another kind is to be created, some other nations will have to assume the responsibility. Only in the English-speaking world will it be possible to find both the will and the power. The United States will most probably emerge as the strongest nation in the world after this conflict; a victorious Britain, even if more weakened by the cost of war, will still be a major world factor. Their combined efforts, democratically directed and supported by other freedom-loving states, could place world peace on a new and firmer basis. Out of such Anglo-American cooperation would come more Canadian-American cooperation.

We cannot be sure, of course, that a will to create a new League or federation of states will exist after the war.

American isolationism might reassert itself. Britain might not desire such a system. Historically the United States has been more ready for intervention abroad than for permanent commitment after intervention. So far American policy, like British policy, has been more concerned with the immediate problem of checking Hitler than with plans for a supra-national authority. Thus far, neither government is committed to a specific post-war program of reconstruction. Yet even if we assume that the United States, despite two examples within a generation of her vital concern in European stability, and despite the increasing range of the aeroplane, should decide to keep clear of European and world collective systems—even so, she is not likely to abandon her policy of hemisphere defense. Indeed, the less there is of a world system, the more need there is of a hemisphere system. So long as this is true, Canadian-American relations are likely to remain close. America's lease of bases in Newfoundland and the West Indies, it must be remembered, is for 99 years.

Out of the present conflict, too, will almost certainly come more planning, both national and regional if not international. The experience in governmental control of total war and total defense is not likely to be cast altogether aside, whatever the ultimate balance may be between the individual and the state. Planning of itself does not produce better international relations; it is a technique rather than a policy, and like man's physical tools can be used for good or ill. American defense and Canada's war effort are for the most part being planned nationally now, and Ogdensburg has as yet made little difference to the economic policies of the two countries. There is a danger that separate defense plans, when firmly established, may place difficulties in the way of future cooperation even though the need for it exists. New vested interests are being created, new plant established which it will be hard to scrap even if uneconomic to maintain. The advantages of continued cooperation have been shown; it is to be hoped that present economic policies will keep in mind these future possibilities. Now, even while the war is on, is the time to begin the planning of a better world. Only if positive action is taken of a forward-looking kind can we be sure that the joint defense agreement between Canada and the United States will really become, in the words of Mr. Mackenzie King, "part of the enduring foundation of a new world order, based on friendship and good will."

# SOME BOOKS FOR FURTHER READING

MacCormac, John. *Canada: America's Problem.* 1940. New York, The Viking Press.

Stacey, C. P. *The Military Problems of Canada.* 1940. Toronto, Ryerson Press.

Dafoe, J. W., edited by. *Canada Fights: An American Democracy at War.* 1941. New York, Farrar & Rinehart.

Scott, F. R. *Canada Today.* A study of her National Interests and National Policy. 1939. London, Oxford University Press.

Callahan, J. M. *American Foreign Policy in Canadian Relations.* 1937. New York, Macmillan.

MacKay, R. A., and Rogers, E. B. *Canada Looks Abroad.* 1938. London, Oxford University Press.

Lower, A. R. M. *Canada and the Far East—1940.* 1940. New York, Inquiry Series, Institute of Pacific Relations.

Dafoe, J. W. *Canada, An American Nation.* 1935. New York, Columbia University Press.

Keenleyside, Hugh L. *Canada and the United States.* 1929. New York, A. A. Knopf.

Fraser, I. F. *The Spirit of French Canada.* 1939. New York, Columbia University Press.

Bovey, Wilfrid. *The French Canadian People Today.* 1938. Toronto, J. M. Dent & Sons.

For detailed studies of various aspects of Canadian-American relations, the reader is referred to the important series of volumes published by the CARNEGIE ENDOWMENT FOR INTERNATIONAL PEACE. Of these, the following deal with matters of contemporary interest:

Angus, H. F. *Canada and Her Great Neighbor.*

Corbett, P. E. *The Settlement of Canadian-American Disputes.*

Ware, N. J., and Logan, H. A. *Labor in Canadian-American Relations.*

Marshall, Herbert, *et al. Canadian-American Industry.*

See also other publications of the CANADIAN INSTITUTE OF INTERNATIONAL AFFAIRS (3 Willcocks Street, Toronto), especially the Contemporary Affairs Series, and the reports of the FOREIGN POLICY ASSOCIATION, 22 East 38th Street, New York City.

## ADDENDA

Since these pages were written further important developments have occurred in Canadian-American relations. They indicate a steadily increasing degree of cooperation as the joint policies of hemisphere defense and aid to Britain are further implemented by the two countries. Space does not allow a detailed examination of all the new developments, but their principal points will be noted.

1. On March 11, 1941 President Roosevelt signed the Lend-Lease Act. This brought United States policy toward the European war still closer to that of Canada, and permitted assistance to Canada as a country whose defense the President "deems vital to the defense of the United States."

2. On March 19 a new St. Lawrence Waterway agreement was signed. It established still another joint body, the Great Lakes-St. Lawrence Basin Commission, composed of ten members, whose function is to supervise the works planned in the International Rapids section of the river. The scheme if carried through will develop an additional 2,700,000 horsepower in the aggregate, and will provide a "deep waterway" with a 27-foot channel throughout the Great Lakes from Montreal to Lake Superior. Besides its commercial advantages, this will enable the shipbuilding plants on the Lakes to be used to build large naval and cargo vessels for use on the high seas. The work on the International Rapids section is estimated to cost $270,000,000, and will take six years to

complete. The terms of the agreement contemplate that it shall be made effective by concurrent legislation of the Canadian Parliament and the Congress of the United States. At the time of writing this has not yet been done. (See above, p. 41–2.)

3. On March 24 the Canadian Parliament was informed that notes had been exchanged between Ottawa and Washington providing a new interpretation of the Rush-Bagot Agreement of 1817 (see above, p. 52). The spirit of the original agreement is maintained, but larger naval vessels are now permitted for training purposes, and armaments may be installed on vessels built in Great Lakes shipyards, if dismantled for the voyage to the sea. This was necessary if the Lakes were to be used for heavy naval shipbuilding.

4. On April 9 was signed the United States-Danish agreement regarding the protection of Greenland. By Article IV the landing fields and defense facilities to be constructed by the United States will be made available to all the American nations "for purposes connected with the common defense of the Western Hemisphere." Thus the principle of sharing of inter-American defense facilities was applied, as in the case of Newfoundland, to another territory adjacent to Canada.  (See above, p. 31–2).

5. On April 18 Colonel O. M. Biggar and Mayor Fiorello H. La Guardia, of the Permanent Joint Board on Defense, announced that strategic plans for the military and naval defenses of the eastern and western coasts of Canada and the United States were complete, and that the Board will in future devote itself to keeping the plans up-to-date to meet changing conditions. In the event of action being necessary "Nothing is left to be done but to put the plan into operation." (See above, p. 58–9.)

6. During the Easter holidays, 1941, Mr. Mackenzie King visited Washington, and Sunday, April 20, he spent at Hyde Park with the President. That evening a joint statement on exchange of defense articles was issued. This conference statement provides an economic corrollary to the Ogdensburg Agreement of the previous August. It announced agreement on the important principle that "in mobilizing the resources of this continent each country should provide the other with the defense articles which it is best able to produce, and, above all, produce quickly, and that production programs should be coordinated to this end." Referring to what he called the "Hyde Park Declaration," Mr. King said of the agreement (Canadian House of Commons, April 28) that "It represents the application to war production of the principle, recognized by Canada and the United States in the trade agreements of peacetime, that the exchange of goods is of mutual benefit."

Specifically, the United States proposed to buy between $200,000,000 and $300,000,000 worth of defense articles from Canada, and to supply her free under the Lend-Lease Act with materials which Canada incorporates in munitions manufactured for Great Britain. Thus the double immediate result will be achieved of easing the strain on the Canadian dollar and increasing total aid to Britain. But, as Mr. King did not fail to point out, "beyond its immediate significance the Hyde Park declaration will have a permanent significance in the relations between Canada and the United States. It involves nothing less than a common plan for the economic defense of the Western Hemisphere." (See above, p. 65 *ff.*)

Revised figures show that Canada's adverse balance of trade with the United States was close to $300,000,000 for

1940. (See above, p. 67). It may well rise to between $400,000,000 and $500,000,000 for 1941. It is not considered likely that the effects of the Hyde Park agreement will so change matters as to enable Canada to ease her restrictions on Canadian travelling in the United States. Canada's total war effort, however, will be much strengthened. In 1940 Canadian-American trade went over the billion dollar mark.

7. Another important move to promote joint economic planning occurred on May 14, when the "Matériel Coordinating Committee" was set up, with two members from each country. Its functions are to exchange vital information on the supplies of strategic raw materials, and to work out the details of cooperation in production. This is not a permanent joint economic committee (see above, p. 45) being for the duration of the war only, but the creation of a permanent committee is reported as being under consideration by the State Department. (*New York Times*, May 15, 1941, p. 10.) It is clear that the steps already taken will make possible a more permanent integration of the economic resources of the North American continent.

*May 20, 1941.*